Rita Dowling

Life is today – live it well

T0160113

Rita Dowling

Life is today
live it well

CELTIC SPIRITUALITY
for
MODERN LIVING

edition EMiL
mitten im leben

With heartfelt thanks to all who inspired
and aided in bringing this book to fruition,
including:

Amy McDonnell-Dowling
Kate McDonnell-Dowling
Anna McDonnell-Dowling
Sharon Young
Dr. Josef Röll
Christa Schuhbauer

Author: Rita Dowling
Text Editor: Sharon Young
Publisher: Dr. Josef Röll

Photography credits:
Page 24:   © Carlo Schrodt/PIXELIO
Page 30:   © carlosh/PIXELIO
Page 52:   fotolia.com © Leah-Anne Thompson #90081
Page 56:   photocase.com © estel

Bibliographische Information Der Deutschen Nationalbibliothek
Die Deutsche Nationalbibliothek verzeichnet diese Publikation in
Der Deutschen Nationalbibliographie;
detaillierte bibliographische Daten sind im Internet über:
http://dnb.ddb.de abrufbar

2nd english edition © 2015 edition EMiL – mitten im leben
edition EMiL is published by J.H. Röll Verlag GmbH, Dettelbach, Germany.

Printed in Germany

ISBN: 978-3-89754-805-3

In Memory of My Parents
Matthew and Ellen Dowling

Ni thugeann an Creann ach a gra
Agus
Is tusa an Creann

The tree knows only love
and
you are the tree

CONTENTS

FOREWORD

Celtic Spirituality seemed to have been forgotten for a long time, so it is a great joy to hold this book from Rita Dowling now in my hands. It is so young and fresh, as if a cool breeze of Irish air is blowing towards me. Some new and unique energy is coming with it and many wonderful ideas. Nevertheless, here speaks an old, timeless wisdom, which managed to stay absolutely clear and powerful right up to this very day.

The book *Celtic Spiritual Wisdom* is able to give us an insight into a tradition which is still alive today, a tradition which can be lived and practised by anybody who wants it. It is a way closely connected with nature; indeed, it grew out of nature itself.

Rita Dowling gives us the essence of Celtic Spirituality in simple and inspiring words. She initiates us into a wisdom which is open for everybody at any time. The language is precise, powerful and vital, as well as poetic and easy to understand. Simple exercises help us to deepen our connection with nature – which is also our own nature – and it is a great pleasure to come to know about the background of the Celtic way of thinking, feeling, and seeing the World.

All existence is alive, creative and new in every moment, and so are we. We are, as Rita Dowling puts it, "Spiritual beings in a Spiritual Universe," and it is a wonderful gift to come to know about this and to experience this deeper and deeper in every moment.

I hope and wish that this book will find many readers, because it provides courage, hope, insight and new ideas. It is a book of great wisdom, beauty and poetry, and it carries the vision of a totally fulfilled life.

Dr. Jochen Niemuth
Founder, The Centre for Meditation and Creativity
Karlstadt, Germany

INTRODUCTION

Celtic Spirituality is re-emerging as a vibrant living spiritual practice in western society. People are once again looking to their roots and ancestry for Spiritual identity and expression.

In the Celtic world there is no duality and the spiritual and natural worlds interact on all levels simultaneously. The earth is honoured and revered with celebrations and rituals at different times in the Celtic calendar.

There is a deep respect for the nature that nourishes us and for the planets and the greater Cosmos that sustains and guides our lives.

We are now in a time of understanding the necessity for sustainable living, both individually and as a collective consciousness. Opportunity now exists to participate in and co-operate with the evolution of Spirit and a renewal of our enchantment with all of life.

PROLOGUE

The light *of morning greets my Spirit*
and
beckons me to the delightful inside me.
Nature inspires me to the natural understanding of who I am
the Creator and the Created.
I agree to participate in this day
coaxed by gentle echoes of the first call.
I breathe life into my thoughts
giving permission for exploration and expansion.
My decision to participate creates the wave of excitement
that rises within me.
Vitality flows and my heart warms
to nourish and nurture
the creation that is me.

To believe that our lives on this wondrous Planet are an endless cycle of suffering and suppression is a denial of our Spiritual essence and the understanding that we are the embodiment of the Divine on Earth.

We are Divine participants in the cosmic well of wonder through our experience and expression of beauty and joy in our daily lives. As creators we determine how we choose to experience and manifest our beliefs about life and its purpose.

We are born out of life force, for life and its glory. In this glorifying of life we come to recognise our connection and participation in the eternal Cosmic web.

Life does not flow by us, but through us, as a fine filter by which we choose to re-present ourselves to our fellow celebrants of life on Earth.

If we can agree that life is a celebration of Heaven on Earth, then we will commit to creating and re-creating the beautiful that is within us all.

CELTIC SPIRITUALITY

The practice of **Celtic Spirituality** invites our daily participation and demonstration of our beauty and joy in the presence of the Sacred.

This understanding gives a reverence to our day and allows our sacredness to determine how we experience life.

The Celtic practitioner invokes the Spiritual vibrations of the Cosmos to bear witness to their day. This acknowledges our responsibility to harmonise with the Sacred elements: Earth, Fire, Air, Water and Ether. Our destiny as spiritual beings is to experience joy, determined by our deep and sacred connection to the Cosmos. In practical terms, this means respect for the Earth from which we suckle, the sky that gives us breath and the Spirit that resides in all.

The practice of **Celtic Spirituality** is the recognition of the Universe as a vibrating, pulsating thought form of which we are the co-creators. It empowers us with the knowledge that we have choice, freedom of thought, capacity for manifestation of our dreams and awareness of our Eternal self.

With this awareness comes our responsibility for our daily lives in thought, word and deed.

Celtic Spirituality, from a modern perspective, recognizes in the sacred Celtic symbol of the **triple spiral** the representation of the cycle of Birth, Death, Rebirth; Body, Mind, Spirit; Maiden, Mother, Crone; the Upperworld, Middleworld, Underworld; the Holy Trinity; and the Conscious, Subconscious, and Super-conscious.

EARTH

When we distress our bodies, we distress our Holy Earth. We are the heartbeat and pulse woven into the fabric of Earth's vibration. Our holy ground breathes life into the forests and meadows and holds the splendour of Heaven on Earth. This it shows us daily in the richness of the artistic display of the rainbow, the colours of light dancing to please us on the faces of flowers and stone.

The colour Earth reflects the harmonics and beauty of the Divine in an unceasing orchestra that gladdens our Soul.

Reverence for Holy ground is awareness with each step we take in our daily life, as we tread on the sacred. The element of Earth is a symbol of our body as the expression of our Great Spirit. We experience our day through the senses of our body: our sight, hearing, smell, taste, and touch. Through our senses we give invitation to our Spirit to dance the day into **Light!**

As our bodies are organic components framed within our Spirit, they cannot be detached from the rhythm and flow of the Cosmos.

To listen to our body is to hear the beat of the primal drum call to wholeness, which is holiness. Our bodies are sensitive to vibrations and instinctively know and inform us when our true rhythm is disturbed. To honour our body is to honour our Spirit with awareness through our senses.

Like the Earth, our bodies hold memories and impressions of our experience. It is, therefore, essential to attend daily to the release of that which does not either serve our Spiritual evolution or keep the natural flow.

Our bodies, like the tree, need good nourishment and tending for fruitful growth. It is vital that we give our body what our Spirit needs. The Cosmic well of wonder is there for our delight, through the channel of our sacred planet.

EARTH is the primal frequency represented by our physical body and the sacred planet that nourishes and sustains us.

Balanced Earth energy is grounding and gives us stamina, strength and a confident energy field.

Too much Earth energy will cause us to be rigid and inflexible in our life situations. It is important to recognise when we need to stand firm and when to let go, just like the great oak and the flexible willow. True listening to our body will bring balance and understanding.

Fear is usually the emotion that brings imbalance to our Earth energy.

The base area and the stomach are associated with the Earth element, as is the entire physical body.

EARTH EXERCISE

Inner Journeying to align with the Earth element, symbol of our physical body.

Create a safe and Sacred space. Make yourself comfortable in a sitting or lying position. Close your eyes and prepare for your Inner journey.

Be aware of your Body and ask your body to: Relax … relax … relax.

Feel all tensions slowly leave your body.

Be aware of your thoughts and ask your Mind to: Relax … relax … relax.

Allow all thoughts to gently flow through you.

Notice your breath, your inhalation of your breath of Life. Relax into the rhythm of your breathing until you feel calm and quiet.

Now visualise that you are walking down a beautiful avenue with trees on either side.

The early morning sunlight is warm on your back. At the end of the avenue is a gate. Slowly open the gate and step inside, closing the gate behind. You have entered a wonderful green meadow. You see the lush grass gently swaying and shimmering in the morning sun. Observe with all your senses the nearby hills, the wild flowers, the birdsong.

In the distance you see a tree and you walk towards it. As you approach, you see it is a magnificent Oak tree. Go to the tree and sit with your back to its trunk. Feel the strength and power of the ancient Oak surround you. Ask permission to merge with its energy for your re-alignment.

As you breathe in, feel yourself melting into the tree. Its branches become your arms; its roots your legs; its trunk your spine, erect and strong. The sap is your Life force.

You and the tree are one, giving and receiving with your breath all that is needed for the nourishment of all. Allow its ancient knowledge to fill you with the glory of who you are. Rest in the belly of the Oak, receiving the Earth's energy from its roots to replenish and nurture your body.

When you feel complete, slowly rise and stand facing the great Oak. Give thanks for all you have received.

Walk slowly back through the meadow to the entrance gate. Turn and gaze at the scene before you. This is the meadow of awareness, and you can visit it at any time you choose for the harmonisation of your body.

Leave the meadow and close the gate behind you. Proceed back along the avenue until you arrive once again in your Sacred space.

Be aware of your body and breathing. Take some time

to absorb your experience and, when you feel ready, open your eyes.

Move your body gently and walk in nature if possible.

Eat and drink a little after your journey to ground your energy body.

The Tree

It appears still in its winter cloak
yet
it celebrates the Heaven beneath the Earth.

Reaches deep into the belly of Life
to nourish and nurture the gift
of Spirit within

that celebrates

the Tree in you
the Tree in me
the *Three* in us

FIRE

Sacred flame,
Inspire me to live with the passion for life in me.
Red blood of my ancestors,
propel me to ignite the flame of consciousness
resting in the belly
of my creation

The sacred element Fire symbolises our enthusiasm for life and the expression of Self. Fire is the energy that nurtures our passion to live the day creatively, with sensitivity and eager participation.

This requires deep attention to listen to our intuition, our spiritual essence. Our inner voice encourages the fire of life in us to radiate our splendour from within out.

There is great freedom and inner power in utilising our creative life force. We hold the key to the door of expression and each individual has a unique gift to share for the benefit of all.

To remain in a place of apathy or denial of self saps the juices of life and curtails the expression of our Spirit in this wondrous Cosmic dance.

FIRE is the element in our physical body which supports our immune system and body temperature. It maintains our general vitality and passion for life. This energy fuels our drive and will power and is the centre of our creativity.

Too much can make us controlling, overpowering and will lead to exhaustion, both mentally and physically

Too little will leave us feeling lethargic and with a lack of enthusiasm for life.

The abdomen and the Heart and liver are associated with this sacred energy.

FIRE EXERCISE

Inner vision to align with the Fire element: Symbol of your passion and destiny.

Create a Sacred space where you will not be disturbed. Light a candle and place it in the middle of this space.

Sit or lie comfortably and close your eyes.

Be aware of your body and allow all tensions to leave your body and: Relax ... relax ... relax.

Let your thoughts flow gently through you and allow them to: Relax ... relax ... relax.

Bring your attention to your breathing. Do not try to alter it, just be attentive to it. Soon you begin to feel a calmness in and around you.

Visualise yourself as part of a large circle of wise beings. They are assisting your alignment with your Fire energy and hold the vision for you.

As the circle opens, you see before you a row of burning

flame. This is the Flame of consciousness and your destiny lies beyond this fire of purification. You are supported by the wise beings.

You prepare yourself with the mantra: I Am the Flame.

Repeat the mantra until you feel ready to embrace the flame and walk through. Your passion for life and understanding of who you are drives you forward through the fire. As you move through, the fire purifies you of restraints in your creative life force and all that does not serve your great Spirit.

When you emerge, you are wrapped in a white robe by the wise beings and invited to lie down in the centre of their circle. The white robe is a symbol of your pure nature, like the white light of the mid-day sun.

You feel your body released and vibrant and your senses clear. In this moment ask the flame of consciousness within you to ignite and show your Divine plan or destiny.

Allow the answer to come to you.

When you have received your insight, slowly stand up, face the wise ones, and give thanks. Step out of the circle and walk back into your Sacred space in this present moment.

Take some time to assimilate the insight received during

your inner vision.

Feel your creative energy rise through you to assist your destiny as a Spiritual being.

It may be necessary after this exercise to eat and drink a little to ground your vibrational body.

Walk in nature, if possible, and remain calm.

CALL OF THE WILD

I spring from my lair, the Wolf within
empowered by the ancient wisdom
of who I am.
Moonglow on my forehead I emerge
to claim the right of passage
beyond the shadow.
I invite you to rise with my Wolf cry
and
embrace the wild forgotten when
you
were the Moon.

WATER

I am the Ocean.
I am the wave of presence
that washes over my day
and
brings to the surface
the
Joy of my Soul

The element Water suggests buoyancy, fluidity and movement.

The Celtic Spirit appreciates the fluidity of our nature. Nothing is static and all is ever changing. To be perceptive and receptive to change gives freedom from the conditioning of our thoughts and feelings.

Our emotions are affected by the water energy. Two thirds of our Planet is influenced by Water. Two thirds of our body is fluidic and therefore responds to the Earth's emotional vibrations. As we nourish our emotions with Divine feelings, we instantly lift our Spirit upwards to experience Love of the Self and Life.

To be emotional (in motion) is to be alive to our sense and sensibility, to distinguish what serves our Spirit in our daily life.

Our emotions guide us and are indicators of our ease or dis-ease with our natural rhythm and surroundings. It is vital to acknowledge and communicate our feelings and allow ourselves the gift of the present.

Our bodies are mainly composed of **WATER**. Just as in nature, water supports all life by cleansing and hydrating our physical body. It represents movement and keeps our emotions fluid and buoyant.

As water knows no boundaries, too much of this energy can cause confusion in our life which can make us unclear and irrational. To balance this energy we need to nurture ourselves with emotions of a higher vibration and give our bodies opportunity for rest and renewal.

The heart is related to this energy and the stomach responds to balance in this area.

WATER EXERCISE

Inner journey to harmonise our emotions with the element of Water.

Create a Sacred space where you will not be disturbed. Sit or lie down in a comfortable position. Close your eyes and be aware of your body.

Allow your body to release all tensions held there and: Relax ... relax ... relax.

Bring your attention to your thoughts and allow your thoughts to gently flow and: Relax ... relax ... relax.

As you slowly relax, bring your attention to your breathing and let go of all outside activity. Relax into your breathing.

In your mind's eye, visualise yourself standing at the top of strong stone steps. There are 10. Start to descend these steps slowly: 1, 2, 3, 4, 5, 6, 7, 8, 9, 10. You are now in front of a large wooden door. Open this door and step inside, closing the door behind you.

You have entered your secret garden of wellness. The scent and fragrance of blossoms fills you with joy. To your right you notice a waterfall flowing into a shimmering pool. You go towards the pool and notice some animals resting beside the pool, enjoying the sunshine. You can see the pool merges with a gentle river that nourishes the surrounding landscape, which is abundant in growth and colour. Remove your garments and step into the warm pool of tranquillity. Feel its texture on your skin. Relax and allow the sacred water to cleanse and release all your old emotions that stagnate you. Become fluid as the water, easy and free.

You are the water of life, buoyant, gracious, generous and flowing.

When you feel ready, step out of the pool. Lie down on the lush grass. Absorb the healing rays of the sun through your inner star, which is located in your stomach. This strengthens you and the physical organs affected by your emotions.

When you feel nourished and balanced, stand up and put on your garments. Once again, be aware of the presence of the animals and the pure love radiating from them. Allow this Love to fill and nurture you

Give thanks for the healing and insight received. Slowly return to the doorway of your garden of wellness. Open this door and step outside, closing the door behind you.

Proceed back up the stone steps, 10, 9, 8, 7, 6, 5, 4, 3, 2, 1, until you arrive back in your physical body. Take three deep breaths . . . Begin to move your body gently.

Allow some time to assimilate your sacred experience.

It is helpful to eat and drink a little after this exercise to ground your energy.

SPIRIT SENSE

Let our eyes see the beautiful
our ears listen only to the bird song.
Let the scent of morning air arouse us
to taste
the nectar of truth on our tongue
and
Let us embrace ourselves,
the beautiful.

AIR

My initiation
into physical form came
with the "inspiration" of my first breath
my agreement
to maintain Mind and Body
with the breath
of
the Eternal

To be in communion with our day inspires transparency of our thoughts and allows Spirit to promote our manifestation of the Divine. The thought is powerful and holds the vibrational energy in the unseen until it ripens to creative form.

Through the energy of **Air**, we enhance our Spiritual growth through knowledge and interaction, relating to all around us, and exploring our senses with our unceasing curiosity and thirst for truth.

To sustain harmony for our beloved Earth requires our attention to our thoughts which create the vibrational attunement for balance. We breathe life into our new thoughts that freshens our mental, calms our nervous centre, and brings clear thinking to our daily life.

When we give ourselves permission to expand our belief systems and cultural ideals, we will all sing the same song.

The nature of the element **AIR** is movement of thought. Just as the wind moves the clouds, so also does the Air frequency give direction to our thoughts and Spiritual growth through knowledge, interaction and how we relate to the World around us.

Balance in this area requires attention to our ideas of life and our breathing.

Over-active thoughts can leave a person restless and nervous and bring about physical conditions like headaches and exhaustion. Breathing is also affected by an imbalance in this element.

The mental and the lungs and abdomen are areas affected by the element of Air.

AIR EXERCISE

Inner Journey to align with the Spiritual element **Air**.

Create a Sacred space where you will not be disturbed.

Sit or lie comfortably and close your eyes.

Be aware of your body, release all tensions held there, and allow your body to: Relax ... relax ... relax.

Notice your thoughts and allow your thoughts to gently flow through you and: Relax ... relax ... relax.

Now bring your attention to your breathing. With each breath you inspire Spirit to guide your breath of life. Slowly your breathing becomes refined and easy. In this moment you begin to feel yourself leave your body and you start to move upwards, out of the room and space you are in.

Continue upwards through clouds and turbulent skies. These represent your lower thoughts and conditions. You continue to journey upwards until you find that you are sitting on a high mountain peak in glorious sunshine under a clear blue sky.

The Air is pure and, as you inhale, it expands your lungs and entire body with the breath of Spirit. You savour this moment and, as you exhale, you release all wrong conditioning from your thoughts.

Now with each in-breath, fill your mind with blue light for calmness and clarity.

Your mind is the Universal Mind. Your thoughts radiate with the Divine vibration and are free to explore the higher realms of consciousness.

You are alert and elated. Slowly you begin to descend through the clouds, down, down into your sacred body and space.

When you feel ready, open your eyes and take a little time to assimilate your journey.

Give thanks for the clarity and balance received.

Take three deep breaths . . . Move your body gently.

It is helpful to eat and drink a little after this exercise to ground your energy.

BREATH OF LIFE

Let my last breath be the eternal thought of Joy
to
fill the space for the next one entering.

ETHER

is the first and last element: It is the great unseen and ever present; the space between the notes; the colours resting in Black and White.

Ether is the silence that speaks when we listen with full awareness, enthusiasm, curiosity and openness to life.

Our Mind is our greatest spiritual essence which enables us to make the unseen seen, to breathe the Ether into reality. This is the art of manifestation.

The unseen is that which is not yet understood and remains in the Ether until knowledge brings it into form.

The realm of Spirit is always supporting and encouraging our expansion and awareness of our Spiritual mind and the all-powerful life force at our disposal in every aspect of our lives.

Listen well with the eye of light and understanding that is within you.

Stillness means presence and when we live in the now, we honour and celebrate the fullness of life. The past fruits have fallen and been ingested in our Spirit. The future fruit has not yet ripened and awaits our arrival. Stillness allows the ripeness of Spirit to flow in its juice to the next moment of ripeness.

Our presence in our day gives acknowledgement to our Spirit to savour what is abundantly around us: LIFE. This is Spirit in reality. A conscious appreciation for the Now gladdens our Soul and brings stillness to our yearning and longing. There is an understanding that life force is necessary for the Now. This is true presence and reverence for our life lived today. Our Spirit does not grow or reside in the past. Only in the present is our Sacred breath required.

In the pause between our breaths, Spirit flows into the moment; therefore, the breath or our conscious intelligence is necessary only for the now. All else is a futile use of our sacred energy.

Invite the stillness in you to assist your appreciation of your life today.

ETHER EXERCISE

Inner silence to attune to higher vibrations:

Prepare a Sacred space where you will not be interrupted.

Sit or lie in a comfortable position and close your eyes. Give attention to your body and allow your body to: Relax… relax… relax.

Bring attention to your thoughts and allow your mental to: Relax… relax… relax.

Now notice your breath and with each breath feel your body and mental becoming calm and quiet. Continue to observe your breathing and notice the pause between your breaths.

In this perfect stillness you inspire Spirit and attune to your inner star. You feel the golden light of spirit enter you and fill your inner star which resides at your breast bone.

Your breath fades into this golden light of perfect love and your star is re-born.

As you feel your inner star expand, visualise it radiating into the Cosmos, connecting to Star streams and galaxies of infinite intelligence. You are one with the Cosmos, a star of Divine creation.

Take some time to bathe in this silent sound of perfection.

Slowly allow your inner star to close its gateway to the Cosmos and bring your awareness to your heartbeat. It is beating to the rhythm of life.

Bring your attention to your body and feel yourself fully present in your physical body, calm and relaxed. Take three deep breaths . . . When you feel ready, open your eyes and relax.

Please take some time to integrate your experience.

It is advisable to ground yourself after this practice by moving your body gently. Eat and drink something light.

AΠGELIC WHISPERS

When Dolphins had wings
and
soared above celestial skies

I watched you
Grace the Heavens,

bathe in the Blue lagoon,
familiar waters of your Creation,

And
I Loved You.

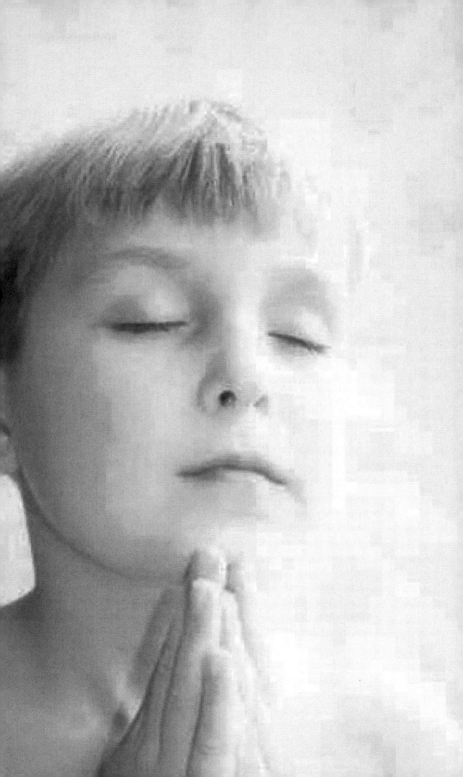

INVOCATION AND BLESSING

Invocation and **Blessing** brings to our day a higher sphere of consciousness to assist our Spirit in its procession through the day. This releases the need to control and diminishes fear.

All is honoured in the Celtic world; each day is a new beginning with opportunity to balance the Universal harmonics and weave the next thread in our daily web of delight.

This is living in present understanding, not in past guilt or future longing.

Our sacred energy is served in the present, and not reserved for the future or imprisoned in the past. To release our past gives life to our present and reverence for our Great Spirit which guides our conscious evolution.

There is no fixed structure or thought in Celtic spiritual belief. An openness to Life and death gives us permission to engage change as part of our creative flow.

Balance is important in our thoughts and emotions. We cannot afford the luxury of an extreme negating philosophy that hinders Spirit's celebration.

Our Mind holds all possibility and the greatness of our Spirit. Our body gives movement to the celebration through dance, sensuality, humour, ritual, creativity and communication.

To disengage our body from our Spirit is to annihilate and deny who we are: Spiritual beings in the wondrous dance of Life. Our bodies, dancing in our Spirit, love life and connect on an intimate and sacred level with nature and the Cosmos.

We and the natural World are One. When we listen to the Spirits of nature, we are uplifted as the natural world, or seen world, mirrors for us our Divine.

The Light of creation is in us and around us. Each time we celebrate our Divine, we re-present ourselves as ambassadors of **Joy** and awaken the ancient force of Creation.

A BLESSING ON YOUR DAY

May you drink from the well of Wonder,
May you speak with the tongue of Truth,
May this moment be your Light to the next.

Forever and ever…..

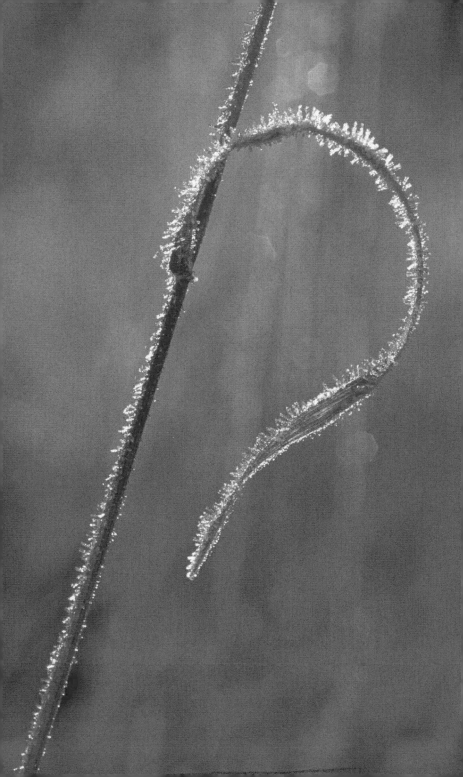

THE VEIL BETWEEN LIFE AND DEATH

With each moment of awareness, we die to our old selves. Each time we relinquish limiting thoughts and patterns, we create space for our Spirit to re-create its splendour and promise. Emptying the mental gives freedom from old trappings that no longer serve who we are.

Spirituality is not sentimentality; it is a process of experiencing joy in the present. It transforms and expands our consciousness through education, contemplation, appreciation and the practical application of our Spirit in reality. Therefore, life only exists through our Soul and is ever expressing itself in and out of our magnificent bodies.

The circle of life is eternal and, therefore, invites us to celebrate and demonstrate the Divine which is within each of us.

Our choices give creation to what we then experience and also how these experiences affect others.

We choose our beliefs of who we are. Our perception creates our experience and when we give attention to this, it quantifies the experience.

When we choose to focus on our abilities, talents and strengths, we give the allowance for our Creative force to provide the necessary situations and opportunity for these gifts to be enjoyed.

Our gifts in this life are the Divine essence which we bring to life through the enhancement of our talents and the sharing of our wonderful in joy.

Our lives as Spiritual beings are a celebration and commitment to dedicate our energy to the Divine within and to align ourselves to the Sacred Spirit for the development of all.

Our experience of ourselves as natural beings, organically formed in unison with the Cosmos, expands our consciousness (awakefullness) to include the non-physical realm as the greater part of our daily Spiritual practice. We utilise our intuition, loving expression, and feelings of higher emotions.

When we live beyond the limitations of our physical senses, we move beyond limiting thoughts of survival and lower instincts. We give our attentive energy to Spiritual experience and exploration for the glory of all.

Sensitivity to our Planet as the body of our Creation that serves us in Love brings empathy and the simple joy of sharing the fruits of our Sacred Earth.

Life is the manifestation of the Divine, the unseen taking form to re-present us, each to the other.

Making the Spiritual practical and the practical Spiritual brings simplicity to its exquisite expression in our otherwise complex World. It enables us to hold the wonder in our daily lives through practice of the Natural Laws of cause and effect.

We are not the effect of Life; we are the FIRST cause. This is the understanding that everything in the magnificent Cosmic web is of our Creation.

With regard to our physical World, we experiment with our Sacredness by processing Life through our vibrational bodies. Each act we perform defines our position in the Divine order of things.

Divining our day is defining our day with awareness of our intuitive selves and our higher purpose in Life.

Spiritual practice is patience in action. Nothing can be forced against the rhythm of Life and the growth of our Soul. When we receive our day with openness and without prejudice, we declare ourselves as Spiritual beings and allow the gate of wonders to open to us.

Life flows through our Mind and Body on vibrational frequencies which we can control to give appropriate action and responses to our daily situations.

An obedience to Natural Law benefits all life: human, animal and plant life. We acknowledge that we live within the perfect Divine order and we are at the core of all life.

Our Spiritual energy guides our day through order and harmony and the portrayal of beauty in our creativity, our bodies and our mentality.

Our day lived well is our life lived well. We choose the moment, we create the Divine thought and we play our part in this great theatre, acknowledging the Wonder of who we are.

TODAY IS LOVE
TOMORROW THE PROMISE

Each day brings the privilege to be creators and to serve, with beauty and joy, the realization of the rainbow in all its glory.

When we reserve Love, we deny our Spirit. Our juices sour and dry up the river of expression to a mere trickle. Love awakens us to ourselves, and from this place of knowing we hold the flame of life up to another. Love is creating the beautiful each day by our decision to experiment with our Divine self and tune to the rhyme and rhythm of our Soul. We are the embodiment of Divine source and this is the planet of exploration of our spiritual essence in physical form. When we no longer require our sensitive and beautiful form, we transcend to the sacred energy of the Spiritual Mind. It is a continuum of our Godliness in the Ethers of the eternal.

It is indeed empowering to embrace responsibility for our daily life. In doing so, we offer ourselves the gift of

the day. Each moment of our day is death and life. As we grow spiritually with each breath, we die to our old selves and move beyond our limitations. Our breath is our agreement, and our thoughts radiate from higher octaves. Our actions carry a grace and ease in knowing that we are weaving a golden thread in the web of our Creation.

Our destiny as Spiritual beings is the experience of Joy, determined by our acknowledgment of our deep and sacred connection with the Cosmos.

In practical terms this means honouring and revering the Earth from which we suckle and respecting the Spirit that resides in all.

Blessing our day sets the tone and tune of our vibrational body. Our words are powerful and **Celtic Spirituality** puts great emphasis on the power of words.

Our communication is our announcement of who we are. A tone of negativity carries a weight that burdens both its creator and the Planet. Recognition of our words as carriers of our Spiritual essence will manifest the beautiful. This is the language of the Soul expressed through our human voice and written words.

Our natural surroundings are exponents of this beauty

and joy. Nature encourages us to break free of our isolation and detachment from the pulse of life. Ever rejoicing and resplendent, it glorifies us through our senses and awakens our hearts.

When we gaze upon nature, we see creation exposing and imposing itself on us.

The sacred elements serve us and present the manifestation of sacred Spirit in reality.

THE PROMISE

I watched the trees stretch their long arms
and
invite a kiss of Spring on their skeleton bones,
allowing her caress after long days bound
to
winter's strict tuition.

Reach up reach out to Ama.
Their bodies awakening to nature's call
Stored wisdom rising like the sap
to the bough.

I watched you, majestic
in the golden Sun.
reach up and call to Ama,

Your voice inviting, allowing the Light
to fill you
with the whisper of Spring
and
the promise of summer.

EPILOGUE

At the core of our Spiritual development is the process of change and awareness through our thoughts, beliefs, patterns and habits. We become fluid and free from framing our lives with the familiar. We hinder ourselves by over-identification with culture, nationalism and tradition which stagnates our Spiritual growth.

Our evolution as Spiritual beings is based on openness to mystery and an expansion of consciousness. This requires a readiness to leave the familiar and comfortable and embrace all of life.

Vision and imagination are a great part of Celtic Spirituality. It encompasses using the heart and mind with clear vision to manifest the highest vibrations of Love and Joy.

As visionaries we hold Sacred space for Spirit and those who follow to walk the Golden circle in the Golden light.

We circle back on ourselves with new awareness and opportunity for the dance of our Spirit. There is no retribution from outside forces, as all is within us. Our inner force compels us through our thoughts, words and deeds to give expression to who we say we are. This can be done through our finite mind or Infinite Mind in each moment. The choice is ours the moment is **NOW**.......

RECOGNITION

I smiled at the golden flower of morning
It showered a thousand rays of thanks on me
for the opportunity

AWARENESS

Was it the rose that stirred the beauty within me

or my own Divine reflected in the rose?

APPENDIX

Poems in the original galic version

(The Tree)

AN CRANN

Samhlaītear go socair ē ina bhrat gheimhridh
ach fōs,
cēiliūrann sē an Neamh faoin dtalamh.

Tēann sē go domhain isteach i mbolg an tsaoil,
chun beathū a thabhairt don rud iontach sin,
an spiorad

a cēiliūrann

an crann ionat
an crann ionam
an triōnōid ionainn

(Call of the Wild)

GLAOCH ŌN FIĀIN

Ēirīm de phreab ō mo fhāir, cosūil le mac tīre,
le cumhacht ionam, ōn gcrīonnacht ārsa,

Taobh thall den scath, tēim amach,
chun ēileamh a dhēanamh ar an slī ceart. . .
solas na gealaī ar m'ēadan.

Tugaim cuireadh duit, ēirī suas in ēineacht le
mo ghlaoch
agus
gach gnē den fhiāin a iniūchadh
a raibh dearmad dēarta ar. . .
nuair a raibh tusa i do ghealach.

(Spirit Sense)

MOTHŪ AN SPIORAD

Go dtugtar cead lenār tsūile an āilleacht a
fheiceāil,
ār gcluasa ēisteacht le ceol na nēan amhāin.

Go dtugtar boladh aer na maidine
spreagadh dūinn
fīrinne an neachtair a bhlasadh ar ār dteanga
agus
beirimid barrōg orainn fēin. . .
an āilleacht.

(Breath of Life)

ANĀIL AN BHEAṪHA

Go dtugtar m'anāil deireanach smaoineamh sīoraī
agus gliondar croī. . .
chun an spās a līonadh, don chēad duine eile.

(Angelic Whispers)

COGAR NA N-AINGIL

Nuair a bhī sciathāin ag na deilf,
agus iad ag ardeitilt os cionn spēartha neamhaī

Bhīos ag faire ort. . .
chomh grāstūil le Neamh

ag snāmh i murlach gorma,
mar chuid den uisce a chruthaīonn tū.

Agus
Bhīos i ngrā leat.

(A Blessing On Your Day)

BEANNACHT AR DO LĀ

Go n-ōlann tū as tobar an iontais,
Go labhrann tū le teanga an fhīrinne,
Go mbeadh an nōimēad seo do sholas
chun leanūint ar aghaidh

Go deo na ndeor ...

(Recognition)

AITHEANTAS

Dēanaim mionghāire ar bhlāth ōir na maidine,
Thug sē solas geal dom,
Agus bhīos fior-buīoch as an deis. . .

(Awareness)

AITHNE

An mhūscail an rōis an āilleacht ionam
nō an ē mo dhiagaire fēin atā ā fheiceāll sa
rōis?

(The Promise)

GEALLTANAS

Bhiōs ag raire ar na crainn, a gcuid lāmha sīnte amach
ag tabhairt cuireadh don Earrach pōg a fhāil
ar a gcuid gcnāmha,
agus iad gafa gach lā leis an gheimhridh crua.

Sīn amach do lāmh do Ama,
glasch an nādur ag dhūiseacht a gcorpanna,
An crionnacht ōn dtaobh istigh ag teacht
chun tusaigh cosūil leis an sū.

Bhīos ag faire ort
agus tū chomh maorga
i scath an ghrian ōir ...
sīn amach do lāmh do Ama.

Do ghuth ag tabhairt cuireadh
agus cead don solas tū fēin a līonadh,
le cogar na n-Earraigh ... agus
gealltanas an tSamhraidh.

BIOGRAPHY

Rita is a native of Dublin, Ireland. She comes from a family of traditional healers and took a natural step into her own healing talent. Her life is a testimony to the challenges facing all of us to grow.

Rita has practiced natural healing since 1990 and has trained in the Philippines with world renowned Spiritual healer Alex Orbito. Rita was initiated in the art of Pranic Healing by Roberto Kastner, founder of The Centro de Terapias Integral, in Madrid, Spain, and in Reiki with Janey Moszniak from the USA. She trained in psychic development with Joan Glennon, who is a medium/clairvoyant in Dublin, Ireland.

Rita is a member of The Irish Association of Transpersonal Psychology

In 1999 she founded "An Scoil Ceiltach Spioradalta" The Celtic Spiritual School in Ireland. This is a centre for creativity and self-development that promotes the growth of the individual as a spiritual being and an integral part of the greater Cosmos.

Rita is an inspirational speaker and spiritual teacher. She conducts lectures and facilitates workshops, healing circles and meditation groups for adults and children in Ireland and throughout Europe.

Rita lives in County Clare, Ireland, with her three daughters.

Publications by Rita Dowling:

"Innen Reisen" (*Inner Journeying*) a series of meditation exercises for young people and adults. (Published in German)

"Leben Ist Heute, Lebe es Gut" (Published in German)

"Inner Journeying" A series of meditation and healing CDs based on the sacred elements of Earth, Fire, Water, Air, and Ether. (Recorded in English)

Forthcoming publications:

Inspirational Calendar, "A Walk Through the Celtic Year"

Set of Celtic Spiritual healing/oracle cards